I0980223

DOVER · THRIFT · EDITIONS

Jewish Wit and Wisdom

EDITED BY
HERB GALEWITZ

DOVER PUBLICATIONS, INC.
Mineola, New York

DOVER THRIFT EDITIONS

GENERAL EDITOR: PAUL NEGRI

Published in Canada by General Publishing Company, Ltd., 895 Don Mills Road, 400-2 Park Centre, Toronto, Ontario M3C 1W3.
Published in the United Kingdom by David & Charles, Brunel House, Forde Close, Newton Abbot, Devon TQ12 4PU.

Bibliographical Note

Jewish Wit and Wisdom is a new work, first published by Dover Publications, Inc., in 2001.

Library of Congress Cataloging-in-Publication Data

Jewish wit and wisdom / edited by Herb Galewitz.
    p. cm.
  ISBN 0-486-41930-4 (pbk.)
   1. Jewish wit and humor. I. Galewitz, Herb.

PN6231.J5 J48 2001
808.88'2'089924—dc21

                      2001032358

Manufactured in the United States of America
Dover Publications, Inc., 31 East 2nd Street, Mineola, N.Y. 11501

Jewish Wit
and Wisdom

The best you get is an even break.

The best part of the fiction in many novels is the notice that the characters are all purely imaginary.

Middle age occurs when you are too young to take up golf and too old to rush up to the net.

Count that day won when, turning on its axis, this earth imposes no additional taxes.

FRANKLIN PIERCE ADAMS

The most popular labor-saving device today is still a husband with money.

If you want to feel important, go on a diet.

A psychiatrist is a fellow who asks you a lot of expensive questions your wife asks for nothing.

Never let a fool kiss you or a kiss fool you.

JOEY ADAMS

A house is not a home.

POLLY ADLER

A woman can be evaluated by her cooking, her dressing— and her husband.

If you don't eat garlic, they'll never smell it on your breath.

Life is a dream for the wise, a game for the fool, a comedy for the rich, a tragedy for the poor.

Adam was the luckiest man: he had no mother-in-law.

If you want to live forever . . . move to our town of Kasrilevka [a town where everyone is poor]. There you can never die, because since Kasrilevka has been a town, no rich man has ever died there.

It's no disgrace to be poor, but it's no great honor, either.

A kind word is no substitute for a piece of herring or a bag of oats.

The real "Jewish Question" is this: From what can a Jew earn a living?

Even if the kugel doesn't quite work out, you still have the noodles.

I have a wife, you have a wife, we all have wives, we've had a taste of paradise, we know what it means to be married.

As we say on Yom Kippur, the Lord decides who will ride on horseback and who will crawl on foot. The main thing is— hope!

SHOLOM ALEICHEM

Change means movement, movement means friction, friction means heat, and heat means controversy. The only place where there is no friction is outer space or a seminar on political action.

SAUL ALINSKY

But it turns out in New York State they have a very funny law that says you can't get a divorce unless you can prove adultery, and that's very strange because the Ten Commandments say, "Thou shalt not commit adultery." So New York State says you have to.

Bisexuality immediately doubles your chances of a date on a Saturday night.

I'm not afraid to die. I just don't want to be there when it happens.

If only God would give me some clear sign, like making a large deposit in my name at a Swiss bank.

Eighty percent of success is showing up.

WOODY ALLEN

Do you have a family tree? We ain't even got a flowerpot.

Summer is the time for those weekend auto trips. One day driving, two days folding the road map.

A bachelor is a man who goes to work every day from a different direction.

Marriage is wonderful. Without it husbands and wives would have to fight with strangers.

MOREY AMSTERDAM

Power corresponds to the human ability not just to act but to act in concert. Power is never the property of an individual; it belongs to a group and remains in existence only so long as the group keeps together.

The hypocrite's crime is that he bears false witness against himself.

HANNAH ARENDT

The best security for old age: respect your children.

It has always been much like writing a check . . . It is easy to write a check if you have enough money in the bank, and writing comes more easily if you have something to say.

SHOLEM ASCH

I do not fear computers. I fear the lack of them.

ISAAC ASIMOV

The best way to lose weight is to eat all you want of everything you don't like.

MAX ASNAS

A political leader must keep looking over his shoulder all the time to see if the boys are still there. If they aren't still there, he's no longer a political leader.

To me, old age is always fifteen years older than I am.

I'm not smart. I try to observe. Millions saw the apple fall but Newton was the one who asked why.

Age is only a number, a cipher for the records. A man can't retire his experience. He must use it. Experience achieves more with less energy and time.

When the outlook is steeped in pessimism I remind myself, "Two and two still make four, and you can't keep mankind down for long."

An elder statesman is somebody old enough to know his own mind and keep quiet about it.

We didn't all come over on the same ship, but we're all in the same boat.

I was the son of an immigrant. I experienced bigotry, intolerance and prejudice, even as so many of you have. Instead of allowing these things to embitter me, I took them as spurs to more strenuous effort.

There are no such things as incurables, there are only things for which man has not found a cure.

BERNARD BARUCH

Marriage always demands the greatest understanding of the art of insincerity possible between two human beings.

VICKI BAUM

Psychoanalysis was a wonderful discovery; it made quite simple people feel they are complex.

S. N. BEHRMAN

If you don't know where you are going, any road will take you there.

DANIEL BELL

Man's life is not a business.

SAUL BELLOW

In Israel, in order to be a realist you must believe in miracles.

DAVID BEN-GURION

Learning begins with listening.

NOAH BEN SHEA

Governments last as long as the undertaxed can defend themselves against the overtaxed.

Between the truth and the search for the truth, I choose the second.

Consistency requires you to be as ignorant today as you were a year ago.

Sexual relationships are often like an hourglass; one single point of contact.

BERNARD BERENSON

Love and romance is something everybody needs and that's irregardless.

After Molly gave Jake some money to go into business, they sat down to dinner and Jake said: "Molly, darling, some day we will be eating out of golden plates." Molly said, "Jake, darling, will it taste any better?"

Not all lovesick maidens are maidens—sometimes they're women, also.

Money is of no consequence unless you owe it.

There are surface differences. To me, the really interesting and beautiful thing is that these surface differences only serve to emphasize how much alike most people are underneath.

GERTRUDE BERG

Women without principle draw considerable interest.

MILTON BERLE

A Pretty Girl Is Like A Melody

IRVING BERLIN

Liberty is liberty, not equality or fairness or justice or human happiness or a quiet conscience.

ISAIAH BERLIN

The materialist is a Calvinist without a God.

EDUARD BERNSTEIN

The man who can smile when things go wrong has thought of someone he can blame it on.

ARTHUR BLOCH

He drinks beer, a habit no more bacchanalian than taking enemas.

MAXWELL BODENHEIM

We suffer primarily not from our vices or weaknesses, but from our illusions. We are haunted, not by reality, but by those images we have put in place of reality.

Nothing is real unless it happens on television.

DANIEL BOORSTIN

Judaism is going to be to American culture what Buddhism was to the eighties. This is going to be the Jewish millenium.

SHMULEY BOTEACH

The greatest menace to freedom is an inert people.

The greatest dangers to liberty lurk in insidious encroachment by men of zeal, well-meaning but without understanding.

We can have democracy in this country or we can have great wealth concentrated in the hands of a few, but we can't have both.

The right to be let alone is the most comprehensive of rights and the right most valued in civilized man.

Behind every argument is someone's ignorance.

Experience teaches us to be most on our guard to protect liberty when the government's purposes are beneficent.

If we would guide by the light of reason, we must let our minds be bold.

I think all of our human experience shows that no one with absolute power can be trusted to give it up even in part.

LOUIS D. BRANDEIS

There's no fool like an old fool—you can't beat experience.

Jacob M. Braude

Men always fall for frigid women because they put on the best show.

I'm a bad voman, but I'm dem good company.

Master Mind! He couldn't Master Mind an electric bulb into a socket.

For $10,000 I'd endorse an opium pipe.

Fanny Brice

Life—the way it really is—is a battle not between Bad and Good but between Bad and Worse.

Joseph Brodsky

Look at Jewish history; unrelieved lamenting would be intolerable. So, for every ten Jews beating their breasts, God designated one to be crazy and amuse the breast beaters. By the time I was five, I knew I was that one.

Max Bialystok (Zero Mostel): Leo, he who hesitates is poor.

(from *The Producers*)

2000-Year-Old Man [on the secret of longevity]: The major thing is I never ever touch fried food. I don't eat it and I wouldn't look at it. And I never run for a bus. There'll always be another.

2000-Year-Old Man: I have 42,000 children and not one comes to visit me.

MEL BROOKS

I'll always be accused of bad taste, especially by people who eat in restaurants that reserve the right to refuse service to anyone.

If you could tell me Christ or Moses, for instance, would say to some kid, "Hey, that's a *white* fountain; you can't drink out of there," you're out of your skull. No one can tell me Christ or Moses would do that.

LENNY BRUCE

When a man has made peace within himself, he will be able to make peace in the whole world.

When a man is intimate with his wife, the longing of the eternal hills wafts about them.

Yet whoever hates directly is closer to a relation than those who are without love and hate.

MARTIN BUBER

You can't help getting older, but you don't have to get old.

The most important thing in acting is honesty. If you can fake that, you've got it made.

Too bad all the people who know how to run the country are busy driving taxicabs and cutting hair.

Happiness is having a large, loving, caring, close-knit family in another city.

GEORGE BURNS

I lived in a pretty tough neighborhood. You either grew up to be a judge or you went to the chair.

Even the great Montezuma, the man who said, "Stop that dancing in the halls" . . . never had a dinner in his honor.

RED BUTTONS

The only thing wrong with immortality is that it tends to go on forever.

The trouble with Oakland is that when you get there it's there.

HERB CAEN

Two dollars will buy all the happiness or all the misery in the world. At least, that used to be the price of a marriage license.

EDDIE CANTOR

There is one difference between a tax collector and a taxidermist—the taxidermist leaves the hide.

MORTIMER CAPLAN

Abstract art? A product of the untalented, sold by the unprincipled to the utterly bewildered.

AL CAPP

Justice is not to be taken by storm. She is to be wooed by slow advances.

Liberty in the most literal sense is negation of law, for law is restraint; the absence of restraint is anarchy.

Justice, though due to the accused, is due to the accuser, too.

Prophecy, however honest, is generally a poor substitute for experience.

BENJAMIN N. CARDOZO

"Kildare? This is Dr. Gillespie. Do you know what you did this morning, you young whelp? You performed an appendectomy with a *milkhidek* scalpel!"

JACK CARTER

Art is the unceasing effort to compete with the beauty of flowers, and never succeeding.

MARC CHAGALL

A definition of law is useful or useless. It is not true or false.

Generally, the theories we believe we call facts, and the facts we disbelieve we call theories.

Legal concepts are supernatural entities which do not have a verifiable existence except to the eyes of faith.

FELIX S. COHEN

The business of the philosopher is well done if he succeeds in raising genuine doubts.

But I still maintain that, by all the canons of our modern books on comparative religion, baseball is a religion, and the only one that is not sectarian but national.

All peoples have pious fictions and sacrosanct expressions which make free thought and honest speech seem improper. This is true even among people noted for their progress in science and technology.

. . . the main function of teaching philosophy should be the opening of the human mind to new possibilities, rather than the inculcation of any new set of doctrines.

Science is a flickering light in our darkness, but it is the only one we have and woe to him who would put it out.

For where the basis of distinction is only the attainment of wealth, everybody tries to appear on a level higher than his own.

Love is a "grand" word that carries a rich afflatus with it; but for the solution of social problems we cannot dispense with the requisite critical intelligence.

MORRIS RAPHAEL COHEN

You can get more with a kind word and a gun than just with a kind word.

IRWIN COREY

If it weren't for pickpockets, I'd have no sex life at all.

RODNEY DANGERFIELD

After I decided to become a Jew, only then did I learn the Jews don't really have all the money. When I found out Rockefeller and Ford were *goyim* I almost resigned.

SAMMY DAVIS, JR.

Judges are the weakest link in our system of justice and they are the most protected.

ALAN DERSHOWITZ

Man doth not live by bread only.

DEUTERONOMY 8:3

Composers shouldn't think too much—it interferes with their plagiarism.

HOWARD DIETZ

Everyone likes flattery; and when you come to royalty you should lay it on with a trowel.

Talk to a man about himself and he will listen for hours.

Description is always a bore, both to the describer and the describee.

"Frank and explicit" is the right line to take when you wish to conceal your own mind and confuse the mind of others.

If you are not very clever, you should be conciliatory.

If you wish to win a man's heart, allow him to confute you.

A precedent embalms a principle.

Plagiarists, at least, have the merit of preservation.

I am bound to furnish my antagonists with arguments, but not with comprehension.

Something unpleasant is coming when men are anxious to tell the truth.

Finality is not the language of politics.

The characteristic of the present age is craven credulity.

Next to knowing when to seize an opportunity, the most important thing in life is to know when to forgo an advantage.

The best way to become acquainted with a subject is to write a book about it.

There are three kinds of lies: lies, damned lies, and statistics.

BENJAMIN DISRAELI

The defects of great men are the consolation of dunces.

Beware the man of one book.

The wise make proverbs and fools repeat them.

Those who do not read criticism will rarely merit to be criticized.

ISAAC D'ISRAELI

The paradox is that those people who left only monuments behind as a record of their existence have vanished with time, whereas the ones who left ideas have survived.

MAX I. DIMONT

History teaches us that men and nations behave wisely once they have exhausted all other alternatives.

ABBA EBAN

To read some of the most important of contemporary writers, one would think they never had a gay moment or that they could not tolerate such a heresy among others.

One of the pet illusions of the reformer and the intellectual is that it is impossible to be serious without being solemn.

IRWIN EDMAN

We should take care not to make the intellect our god; it has, of course, powerful muscles, but no personality.

Neither can I believe that the individual survives the death of his body, although feeble souls harbor such thoughts through fear or ridiculous egotism.

Never did Mozart write for eternity, and it is for precisely that reason that much of what he wrote is for eternity.

I never think of the future. It comes soon enough.

I am absolutely convinced that no wealth in the world can help humanity forward, even in the hands of the most devoted worker in this cause . . . Money only appeals to selfishness and irresistibly invites abuse. Can anyone imagine Moses, Jesus, or Gandhi armed with the moneybags of Carnegie?

The important thing is not to stop questioning.

God is subtle—but he is not malicious.

Peace cannot be kept by force. It can only be achieved by understanding.

Nationalism is an infantile disease. It is the measles of mankind.

Truth is what stands the test of experience.

When a man sits with a pretty girl for an hour, it seems like a minute. But let him sit on a hot stove for a minute—and it's longer than any hour. That's relativity.

The discovery of nuclear chain reaction need not bring about the destruction of mankind any more than the discovery of matches.

Science without religion is lame, religion without science is blind.

Common sense is the collection of prejudices acquired by age eighteen.

Imagination is more important than knowledge.

It is easier to denature plutonium than to denature the evil spirit of man.

Few people are capable of expressing with equanimity opinions which differ from the prejudices of their social environment.

I cannot believe that God plays dice with the cosmos.

The only rational way of educating a child is to be an example—of what to avoid, if one can't be the other sort.

Perfection of means and confusion of goals seem, in my opinion, to characterize our age.

If you are out to describe the truth, leave elegance to the tailor.

The most incomprehensible thing about the world is that it is comprehensible.

The process of scientific discovery is, in effect, a continual flight from wonder.

ALBERT EINSTEIN

A wide knowledge of men and events seems to me necessary to the artist, but participation and action in political events and movements must remain a matter of personal predilection.

JACOB EPSTEIN

A sound marriage is not based on complete frankness; it is based on a sensible reticence.

The shoulders of a borrower are always a little straighter than those of a beggar.

MORRIS L. ERNST

Millions long for immortality who do not know what to do with themselves on a rainy Sunday afternoon.

SUSAN ERTZ

If you give up wearing glasses you look better but you don't see as well.

EVAN ESAR

A good memory is one trained to forget the trivial.

Ennui, felt on the proper occasions, is a sign of intelligence.

Miss [Gertrude] Stein was a past master in making nothing happen very slowly.

CLIFTON FADIMAN

Switzerland: beautiful but dumb.

Being an old maid is like death by drowning, a really delightful sensation after you cease to struggle.

A woman can look both moral and exciting—if she also looks as if it was quite a struggle.

EDNA FERBER

If your husband likes gefilte fish, don't shove fried fish down his throat and say: "You dope, you don't know what good is."

DAILY FORWARD

Parents can only give good advice or put them in the right paths, but the final forming of a person's character lies in their own hands.

ANNE FRANK

If facts are changing, the law cannot be static.

If err we must, let us err on the side of tolerance.

But as judges we are neither Jew nor gentile, neither Catholic nor agnostic. We owe equal attachment to the Constitution and are equally bound by our judicial obligations whether we derive our citizenship from the earliest or the latest immigrants to these shores.

If one faith can be said to unite a great people, surely the ideal that holds us together beyond any other is our belief in the moral worth of the common man, whatever his race or religion.

One who belongs to the most vilified and persecuted minority in history is not likely to be insensible to the freedom guaranteed by our Constitution.

People listen to a large extent because of vacuity of mind.

To some lawyers all facts are created equal.

FELIX FRANKFURTER

In a normal sex life no neurosis is possible.

It has seemed to us that the pleasure of wit originates from an economy of expenditure in inhibition, of the comic from an economy of expenditure in thought, and of humor from an economy of expenditure in feeling.

Men are generally not candid in sexual matters. They do not show their sexuality freely, but they wear a thick overcoat—a fabric of lies—to conceal it, as though it were bad weather in the world of sex.

SIGMUND FREUD

Inflation is the one form of taxation that can be imposed without legislation.

Political freedom . . . is a necessary condition for the long-term maintenance of economic freedom.

Concentrated power is not rendered harmless by the good intentions of those who create it.

MILTON FRIEDMAN

It is not good that the man should be alone.

GENESIS 2:18

I will make of thee a great nation, and I will bless thee, and make thy name great.

GENESIS 12:2

Because systems of mass communications can communicate only officially acceptable levels of reality, no one can know the extent of the secret unconscious life. No one in America can know what will happen. No one is in real control.

ALLEN GINSBERG

She was a singer who had to take any note above A with her eyebrows.

MONTAGUE GLASS

If all the seas were ink, and all the reeds pens, and all the people scribes, it would not be enough to record all the misfortunes of the Jews in a single year.

GLOSS (c. 1400) to the *Megillat Taanit*

If a girl doesn't watch her figure, the boys won't.

PAULETTE GODDARD

Law not served by power is an illusion, but power not ruled by law is a menace.

Modern diplomats approach every problem with an open mouth.

ARTHUR GOLDBERG

To talk music without hearing it is about as fruitful as to sit in an Eveless desert discussing the beauty of women.

Civilization may be fastidious; Nature is not.

Diplomacy is to do and say
The nastiest thing in the nicest way.

Man pays for specialization; in his attempt to conquer the part he loses contact with the whole and bereft of this sense of entireness, he is left to contemplate, rather uneasily, a sheaf of brilliant fragments.

ISAAC GOLDBERG

I'm the guy . . .

A touch of art may nourish the soul, but a good laugh always aids the digestion.

Influence is like a carpet or wallpaper or a dog's tail. It's good to have it there, but it's also good not to call too much attention to it.

RUBE GOLDBERG

No great idea in its beginning can ever be within the law. How can it be within the law? The law is stationary. The law is fixed. The law is a chariot wheel which binds us all regardless of conditions or place or times.

Idealists . . . foolish enough to throw caution to the winds . . . have advanced mankind and have enriched the world.

EMMA GOLDMAN

Get yourself a few stars, a well-known author, and a competent director, and you have the mucus of a good picture.

Anybody who goes to see a psychiatrist ought to have his head examined.

Too caustic? To hell with the cost! We'll make the picture anyway.

In two words: im-possible.

SAMUEL GOLDWYN

Let your child hear you sigh every day; if you don't know what he's done to make you suffer, *he* will.

Spock, shlock, don't talk to me about that stuff. A man doesn't know how to bring up children until he's been a mother.

DAN GREENBURG

Oohoo!—sotch a dollink baby! Ate opp all de oatmill.

Go prectise queeck on de wiolin or I'll geeve you dot you'll wouldn't know from where it came from—.

MILT GROSS

Poor people know poor people and rich people know rich people. It is one of the few things La Rochefoucauld did not say, but then La Rochefoucauld never lived in the Bronx.

MOSS HART

Trying to determine what is going on in the world by reading newspapers is like trying to tell the time by watching the second hand of a clock.

A man of any age can persuade himself that a woman's thighs are altar rails and that her passion is the hosanna of virtuous love rather than the wanton tumult of nerve endings.

The rule in the art world is: you cater to the masses or you kowtow to the elite; you can't have both.

BEN HECHT

No matter what side of an argument you're on, you always find some people on your side that you wish were on the other side.

JASCHA HEIFETZ

Experience is a good school, but the fees are high.

He who for the first time loves,
Even vainly, is a God.
But the man who loves again,
And still vainly, is a fool.

God will forgive me; that's his business.

To love and be loved—this
On earth is the highest bliss.

I will not say that women have no character; rather, they have a new one every day.

The Romans would never have found time to conquer the world if they had been obliged first to learn Latin.

I cannot relate my own griefs without the thing becoming comic.

HEINRICH HEINE

Cynicism is an unpleasant way of saying the truth.

LILLIAN HELLMAN

The course of life is unpredictable . . . no one can write his autobiography in advance.

Our concern is not how to worship in the catacombs but how to remain human in the skyscrapers.

It is of the essence of virtue that the good is not to be done for the sake of a reward.

ABRAHAM JOSHUA HESCHEL

The difference between wife and mistress is the difference between night and day.

New York is a city where everyone mutinies but no one deserts.

HARRY HERSHFIELD

What is hateful to you, do not to your fellow man: that is the whole Law; all the rest is interpretation.

If I am not for myself, who will be for me? And if I am only for myself, what am I? And if not now—when?

HILLEL

Politics is the science of who gets what, when and why.

SIDNEY HILLMAN

Smelling like a municipal budget.

I play with the bulls and the bears;
I'm the Bartlett of market quotations.

Breathes there a man with soul so tough
Who says two sexes aren't enough?

SAMUEL HOFFENSTEIN

For they have sown the wind, and they shall reap the whirlwind.

HOSEA 8:7

Tsu brach a fuss (break a leg), *tsu brach badderen fessen* (break both legs)—which means you will have no kick coming.

WILLIE HOWARD

The suburban Jews . . . lived with whatever remnants of their youthful experience they could salvage, and "bagels and lox" were part of what they still had left, tokens of the past to which they clung partly because it reminded them of all that was gone.

IRVING HOWE

. . . and they shall beat their swords into plowshares, and their spears into pruning-hooks; nation shall not lift up sword against nation, neither shall they learn war any more.

ISAIAH 2:4

Woe unto them that are wise in their own eyes, and prudent in their own sight!

ISAIAH 5:21

How beautiful upon the mountains are the feet of him that bringeth good tidings, that publisheth peace.

ISAIAH 52:7

Cities are full of people with whom a certain degree of contact is useful and enjoyable, but you do not want them in your hair. And they do not want you in theirs either.

JANE JACOBS

I should of stood in bed.

JOE JACOBS

I know Governor Thomas E. Dewey and Mr. Dewey is a fine man. So is my Uncle Morris. My Uncle Morris shouldn't be president, and neither should Dewey.

If you haven't struck oil in five minutes, stop boring.

Marriage is a mistake every man should make.

GEORGE JESSEL

Man that is born of a woman is of few days, and full of trouble.

JOB 14:1

A book must be an ice-axe to break the seas frozen inside our soul.

You can hold back from the suffering of the world, you have free permission to do so, and it is in accordance with your nature, but perhaps this very holding back is the one suffering you could have avoided.

Jewishness is not merely a question of faith, it is above all a question of the practice of a way of life in a community conditioned by faith.

Only our concept of time makes it possible for us to speak of the Day of Judgment by that name; in reality it is a summary court in perpetual session.

The meaning of life is that it stops.

You are free and that is why you are lost.

Perhaps there is only one cardinal sin: impatience. Because of impatience we were driven out of Paradise; because of impatience we cannot return.

FRANZ KAFKA

The kind of doctor I want is one who, when he's not examining me, is home studying medicine.

My friend Mitzic swallowed a candle—so I asked him, "Did the paraphernalia?"

One man's Mede is another man's Persian.

How many persons, even among your best friends, really hope for your success on an opening night? A failure is somehow so much more satisfying all around.

I never want to go anyplace where I can't get back to Broadway and Forty-Fourth by midnight.

Anyone who can afford to own a hundred thousand dollars' worth of jewels can afford to have them stolen.

A man had two daughters, Lizzie and Tillie. Lizzie is all right, but you have no idea how punctilious.

I saw the play at a disadvantage—the curtain was up.

Posterity is just around the corner

GEORGE S. KAUFMAN

Mrs. Potter (Margaret Dumont): I don't think you'd love me if I were poor.
Mr. Hammer (Groucho Marx): I might, but I'd keep my mouth shut.

GEORGE S. KAUFMAN AND MORRIE RYSKIND (from *The Cocoanuts*)

Captain Spaulding (Groucho Marx): One morning I shot an elephant in my pajamas. How he got into my pajamas I don't know.

GEORGE S. KAUFMAN, MORRIE RYSKIND, BERT KALMAR
AND HARRY RUBY (from *Animal Crackers*)

The nice thing about being a celebrity is that when you bore people, they think it's their fault.

You can't win through negotiations what you can't win on the battlefield.

Power is the ultimate aphrodisiac.

HENRY KISSINGER

A coward is a hero with a wife, kids and a mortgage.

MARVIN KITMAN

Boos and hisses have a greater degree of honesty than applause.

JAKOB KLATZKIN

What can you say about a society that says that God is dead and Elvis is alive?

IRV KUPCINET

What I am waiting for is a movie about beautiful quintuplets who love the same man.

HARRY KURNITZ

The prophet, the preacher, the politician have distant goals; distant and often obscure. . . . Only we, the aesthetes, have no goals and no purposes. . . . The tree blooms—the tree is beautiful . . . Everything that is here is beautiful; and because it is here. This is the truth known to all who live with their senses.

ZISHA LANDAU

Opportunities are usually disguised as hard work, so most people don't recognize them.

ANN LANDERS (EPPIE LEDERER)

. . . "Give me your tired, your poor,
Your huddled masses yearning to breathe free,
The wretched refuse of your teeming shore.
Send these, the homeless, tempest-tost to me,
I lift my lamp beside the golden door."

EMMA LAZARUS

Children give life to the concept of immaturity.

The left succeeds in forcing country clubs to operate as if they were the source of some necessary municipal service. The left should pay more attention to which Democratic president is sending his daughter to private school than which private club does not admit women, or blacks or Jews.

Being a woman is of special interest only to aspiring male transsexuals. To actual women, it is simply a good excuse not to play football.

Ask your child what he wants for dinner only if he's buying.

Brown rice is ponderous, overly chewy, and possessed of unpleasant religious overtones.

If your sexual fantasies were truly of interest to others, they would no longer be fantasies.

There is a credit card that enables you to get $50,000 cash anywhere in the world. I haven't the slightest idea as to what sort of emergency would require $50,000 in cash, other than a ransom demand.

There is no such word as *actualize*. There is no such word as *internalize*. There is, in fact, but one instance where the letters *ize* are appropriate here and that is in the word *fertilize*.

FRAN LEBOWITZ

[To a bad Boston audience] If I was Paul Revere, I'd never have warned you.

JACK E. LEONARD

Everyone wonders what a man who never says anything sounds like.

I once said David Susskind's prose is dipped in chicken fat.

Happiness isn't something you experience; it's something you remember.

An epigram is only a wisecrack that's played Carnegie Hall.

Strip away the phony tinsel of Hollywood and you find the real tinsel underneath.

A pun is the lowest form of humor—when you don't think of it first.

OSCAR LEVANT

No matter how well a toupee blends in back, it always looks like hell in front.

Insanity is hereditary; you can get it from your children.

You Don't Have To Be In Who's Who *To Know What's What*

We usually meet all our relatives only at funerals where someone always observes, "Too bad we can't get together more often."

You must learn from the mistakes of others. You can't possibly live long enough to make them all yourself.

SAM LEVENSON

Statistics are like a bikini. What they reveal is suggestive, but what they conceal is vital.

AARON LEVENSTEIN

Reading, reflection and action based upon reflection can make you a better person and you can change the world.

RICHARD C. LEVIN

Chicago—a pompous Milwaukee.
Cleveland—two Hobokens back to back.

Book—what they make a movie out of for television.

He is a fine friend. He stabs you in the front.

LEONARD LOUIS LEVINSON

The humble digger of the earth may be a slave in body; the young business man or engineer who furthers the interests of his master is a slave in soul.

So long as there is discrimination, there is exile.

No man who has been young in the deep and true sense can render into words the scene of his youth.

The passion of love is the central passion of human life. It should be humanized; it should be made beautiful.

True justice need not be tempered by mercy. It excludes the necessity for mercy. You do not need to be merciful until you have ceased to be just . . . !

Missionary work—the feeble impudence of teaching other races a set of legends and a bankrup system of conduct.

The world is wide and its paths are many and the fate of no man is quite his own to shape.

To be a Jew is to be a friend of mankind, to be a proclaimer of liberty and peace.

Art . . . is not what you suppose: it's not a game—like bridge; it's not a ceremony—like a reception. It is the record and clarification of deepest human experience.

We shall not have lovelier private morals until we have destroyed public morality—the fang and claw of Puritan capitalism.

LUDWIG LEWISOHN

Freedom of the press is limited to those who own one.

A. J. LIEBLING

Give your child truth as well as respect; prepare him for the world as it is—a complex reality of good, bad and indifferent.

This is the revolution that is needed in our age—the understanding that we ought to be far more unhappy about remaining on the kindergarten level of conscience than about remaining on the childish level of information and intellect.

Life is not paradise. It is pain, hardship, failure and temptation shot through with radiant gleams of light, friendship and love.

JOSHUA LOTH LIEBMAN

Propaganda is that branch of lying which often deceives your friends without ever deceiving your enemies.

Where all think alike, no one thinks very much.

The principle of majority rule is the mildest form in which force of numbers can be exercised. It is a pacific substitute for civil war.

The genius of a good leader is to leave behind him a situation which common sense, without the grace of genius, can deal with successfully.

Whereas each man claims his freedom as a matter of right, the freedom he accords to other men is a matter of toleration.

The only dependable foundation of personal liberty is the personal economic security of private property.

The justification of majority rule in politics is not to be found in its ethical superiority.

WALTER LIPPMAN

Gary Cooper and Greta Garbo may be the same person. Have you ever seen them together?

ERNST LUBITSCH

Success is that old ABC—ability, breaks and courage.

CHARLES LUCKMAN

To remember much is not necessarily to be wise.

SAMUEL DAVID LUZZATTO

I seem to be alone in finding J.D. Salinger no more than the greatest mind to stay in prep school.

Norman Mailer

Man's obsession to add to his wealth and honor is the chief source of his misery.

Prayer without devotion is not prayer. If a man pray without devotion, he should repeat his prayer with devotion.

No man ever became poor through giving charity, and no evil or harm was ever caused through the giving of charity.

A truth does not become greater by repetition.

Strengthen ye the weak hands and confirm the feeble knees . . . Know that this is the true Divine Law given us by the chiefest of all the prophets first and last and by this Law we have been set apart from all men, not for our deserts but because of His loving kindness and bounty.

We are not the center of the universe, neither you and I as individuals, nor the whole human race as such. The universe must be considered as one whole of interrelated parts and its purpose is not our puny selves.

God in his essence cannot be known; all that we can know of him is through his acts; his acts are to be seen both in his visible handiwork, the created world, which it is our duty to study, and in his moral activity which it behooves us to imitate.

Those who have succeeded in finding a proof for everything that can be proved, who have a true knowledge of God so far as a true knowledge can be attained, and are near the truth wherever an approach to the truth is possible, they have reached the goal, and are in the palace in which the King lives.

Maimonides

Paris, where half the women are working women and half the women are working men.

Derely Devore, the star, rose from the chorus because she was cool in an emergency—and warm in a taxi.

A final draft is what you put in the typewriter the night before it is due.

She could give you an eyewitness account of the Crucifixion and put you to sleep.

The play needs only the addition of a couple of nicely fried eggs to pass anywhere as America's favorite dish.

HERMAN MANKIEWICZ

To speed up the Second Front we will from now on be forced to sell our farmer cheese in quantities of no less than half a pound.

Only hear me, believe: Let them charge a dime, let them charge a dollar, let them grind it fine and let them grind it coarse—but sonny, kiddo, all . . . talcum powder . . . is The Same!

President Roosevelt had a hundred days, but you got till this Monday to enjoy such savings on our Farm Girl Pot Cheese.

WALLACE MARKFIELD

If a song writer is ethical, he will not cop a tune within three years of its publication.

EDWARD B. MARKS

Whoever named it necking was a poor judge of anatomy.

I went into show business because my mother's brother was Al Shean. He was netting $250 a week (sans taxes) and I quickly decided that if this kind of money was laying around in show business I was going to get a piece of it.

Dear Chico: . . . In the meantime, always examine the dice.

Wives are people who feel that they don't dance enough.

One of the best hearing aids a man can have is an attentive wife.

GROUCHO MARX

From each according to his abilities, to each according to his needs.

KARL MARX

Bathos is pathos after too many drinks.

PATRICIA MARX

A Jew on a vacation is just looking for a place to sit. A Jew sees a chair, it's a successful vacation.

Congress doesn't care. They get paid whether the country makes money or not. I say put them on commission.

I have enough money to last me the rest of my life, unless I buy something.

When a Jew has a boat he only says one thing. "I sleep six. I sleep twelve. I sleep thirty-eight. I sleep, I sleep . . ." To him it's not a boat, it's a dormitory.

JACKIE MASON

We Jews have a secret weapon in our struggle with the Arabs—we have no place to go.

Whether women are better than men I cannot say—but I can say that they are no worse.

GOLDA MEIR

Predictions of greatness in the world of show business are usually, to borrow a few similes from the world of plant life, as sweet as the pomegranate and as impassioned as the orchid; as perishable as the crocus, as sticky as the flytrap and as common as the dandelion.

GILBERT MILLSTEIN

Be honest with yourself 'til the end of your life. Then listen to the slow movement of the Schubert Quintet and kick the bucket.

NATHAN MILSTEIN

Simba, those jungle drums are driving me mad . . . What are they saying—what, what, what? "They say, 'You no have to be Jewish to enjoy Levy's bread!'"

JAN MURRAY

A beautiful young lady is an accident of nature. A beautiful old lady is a work of art.

LOUIS NIZER

From Coney Island to the cemetery, it's the same subway—
it's the same fare.

GRACE PALEY

You call this a script? Give me a couple of $5,000-a-week
writers and I'll write it myself.

JOE PASTERNAK

Vas you dere, Sharlie?

JACK PEARL

MEN: Why worry? See Dr. Morty Perelman, night or day—
no more expensive than any quack.

S. J. PERELMAN

It is not enough to write in Yiddish; one must have
something to say.

Y. L. PERETZ

Love is nothing more perhaps than the stimulation of those
eddies which, in the wake of an emotion, stir the soul.

We are healed of a suffering only by experiencing it to the
full.

MARCEL PROUST

A virtuous woman is a crown to her husband.

PROVERBS 12:4

Better is a dry morsel, and quietness therewith, than an house full of sacrifices with strife.

PROVERBS 17:1

A good name is rather to be chosen than great riches, and loving favor rather than silver and gold.

PROVERBS 22:1

Train up a child in the way he should go; and when he is old he will not depart from it.

PROVERBS 22:6

Where there is no vision, the people perish.

PROVERBS 29:18

Blessed is he that considereth the poor.

PSALM 41:1

So teach us to number our days, that we may apply our hearts unto wisdom.

PSALM 90:12

Man is like to vanity: his days are as a shadow that passeth away.

PSALM 144:4

Don't make a megillah out of every little thing.

MAE QUESTAL

I base most of my fashion taste on what doesn't itch.

GILDA RADNER

I always thought when you got older, you got wiser. Well, it doesn't help. You know what it is all about, but don't let anybody tell you that lessens the pain.

It is impossible to break the heart of a young, beautiful and healthy woman.

SAMSON RAPHAELSON

If all the world were on the rocks
And I alone in clover,
I'd open wide my door and bid
The sorry world come over.

I write my songs through many a dark night,
Choosing my rhymes like jewels, rare and bright.
In all those nights they flamed upon the dark
But on my life they never shed one spark.

ABRAHAM REISEN

Canadians represent, as it were, the least militant North American minority group. The white, Protestant, heterosexual ghetto of the North.

MORDECAI RICHLER

The media, far from being a conspiracy to dull the political sense of the people, could be seen as a conspiracy to disguise the extent of political indifference.

DAVID RIESMAN

A love song is just a caress set to music.

SIGMUND ROMBERG

Never mind what they say about you in a newspaper. Tomorrow someone will wrap a herring in it.

Does the Spearmint Lose its Flavor on the Bedpost Overnight?

Never invest your money in anything that eats or needs repainting.

I believed what everybody believed in 1922—that U.S. Steel would hit 500, that nice girls didn't kiss the first time you took them out, and that Heaven was not for Democrats.

BILLY ROSE

The Sexual Revolution: Conquest of the last frontier, involving the efficient management and manipulation of reproductive organs for the purpose of establishing the New Puritanism.

Free enterprise: A huge area of the American economy still noticeable to observers with peripheral vision after they subtract the public sector, conglomerates, federally supported agriculture, monopolies, duopolies and oligopolies.

BERNARD ROSENBERG

The defense seems to have been prepared according to the old rules. "If facts are against you, hammer the law. If the law is against you, hammer the facts. If the facts and the law are against you, hammer opposing counsel."

JACOB J. ROSENBLUM

Every man learns to live. But by that time, he is seventy years of age at least.

PAUL ROSENFELD

When you have a lemon, make lemonade.

JULIUS ROSENWALD

Two Jews on an island will build three synagogues—one for each, and a third neither wants to attend.

No man who hates dogs and babies can be all bad.

LEO ROSTEN

White bread, rye bread
Pumpernickel, challah
All those for Weequahic,
Stand up and hollah!

PHILIP ROTH

Making music is like making love: the act is always the same, but each time it is different.

What good are vitamins? Eat a lobster, eat a pound of caviar—live! If you are in love with a beautiful blonde with an empty face and no brains at all, don't be afraid. Marry her! Live!

ARTUR RUBINSTEIN

Sleep without a pillow or allow yourself a flat one only. This wards off extra chins.

HELENA RUBINSTEIN

To be a Jew in the twentieth century
Is to be offered a gift. If you refuse,
Wishing to be invisible, you choose
Death of the spirit, the stone insanity.

MURIEL RUKEYSER

Humility is the worst form of ego. It's usually indulged in by people who can afford it—"He's a wonderful guy, so humble, this millionaire."

Jesse Jackson is a man of the cloth. Cashmere.

Washington couldn't tell a lie, Nixon couldn't tell the truth, and Reagan couldn't tell the difference.

MORT SAHL

For others a knowledge of the history of their people is a civic duty, while for the Jews it is a sacred duty.

MAURICE SAMUEL

Do you recall the cable that the Elman family sent out from Moscow when the great violinist was born? It read: "Mischa accomplished."

M. LINCOLN SCHUSTER

Only the past is immortal.

Even paranoids have real enemies.

Existentialism means that no one else can take a bath for you.

DELMORE SCHWARTZ

It's possible to own too much. A man with one watch knows what time it is; a man with two watches is never quite sure.

LEE SEGALL

I got a religion that wants to take heaven out of the clouds and plant it right here on the earth where most of us can get a slice of it.

IRWIN SHAW

Zeppo Marx: Dad, the garbage man is here.
Groucho Marx: Tell him we don't want any.

Chico Marx: I would like to say good-bye to your wife.
Groucho Marx: Who wouldn't?

AL SHEAN (from *Home Again*)

Never criticize a guy for something you do yourself.

Any bum who can't get drunk by midnight ain't tryin'.

TOOTS SHOR

[Headline, *Variety*, October 1929] WALL STREET LAYS AN EGG

SIME SILVERMAN

Happy is the man that findeth wisdom and the man that getteth understanding.

SOLOMON

Riches, Fame and Pleasure. With these three the mind is so engrossed that it can hardly think of any other good.

No one should expect the government to act in accordance with the moral code appropriate to the conduct of the individual.

The world would be happier if men had the same capacity to be silent that they have to speak.

Nature abhors a vacuum.

It is a comfort to the unhappy to have companions in misery.

Fear cannot be without hope nor hope without fear.

If you want the present to be different from the past, study the past.

The basis of wisdom is not in the reflection on death but in the reflection on life.

Man is a social animal.

If the State acts in ways abhorrent to human nature, it is the lesser evil to destroy it.

There is no such thing as free will. The mind is induced to wish this or that by some cause, and that cause is determined by another cause, and so on back to infinity.

BARUCH SPINOZA

[On Oakland] When you get there, there isn't any there there.

I like familiarity. In me it does not breed contempt. Only more familiarity.

Money is always there but the pockets change; it is not in the same pockets after a change, and that is all there is to say about money.

Generally speaking anybody is more interesting doing nothing than doing anything.

In the United States, there is more space where nobody is than where anybody is. This is what makes America what it is.

Rose is a rose is a rose is a rose.

GERTRUDE STEIN

Experience—a comb life gives you after you lose your hair.

JUDITH STERN

Success to me is having ten honeydew melons and eating only the top half of each one.

Why does a woman work ten years to change a man's habits and then complain that he's not the man she married?

BARBRA STREISAND

A cartload of pasteurized milk for nurslings at four o'clock in the morning represents more service to civilization than a cartful of bullion on its way from the Sub-treasury to the vaults of a national bank five hours later.

People who want to understand democracy should spend less time in the library with Aristotle and more time on the buses and in the subway.

SIMEON STRUNSKY

I cannot give you the formula for success, but I can give you the formula for failure—which is: Try to please everybody.

HERBERT BAYARD SWOPE

He who has fed a stranger may have fed an angel.

Be ever soft and pliable like a reed, not hard and unbending like a cedar.

Examine the contents, not the bottle.

The noblest charity is to prevent a man from accepting charity; and the best alms are to show and enable a man to dispense with charity.

TALMUD

Judicial restraint is but another form of judicial activism.

LAURENCE H. TRIBE

When it comes to Chinese food . . . the less known about the preparation the better.

It has finally dawned on me that my wife and I got married during that awkward period in the history of domestic relations between dowries and prenuptial agreements.

CALVIN TRILLIN

Snobbery is pride in status without pride in function.

. . . literature is the human activity that takes the fullest and most precise account of variousness, possibility, complexity, and difficulty.

Immature artists imitate. Mature artists steal.

LIONEL TRILLING

I've been rich and I've been poor. Believe me, rich is better.

SOPHIE TUCKER

Having the critics praise you is like having the hangman say you've got a pretty neck.

ELI WALLACH

When asked how far engaged couples should go, Farnsworth himself replied that those in the metropolitan area should go as far as Union City, New Jersey.

IRA WALLACH

The world is divided into two groups of nations—those which want to expel the Jews and those which do not want to receive them.

If a man has a piece of something in his eye, he doesn't want to know whether it's a piece of mud or a piece of gold. He just wants to get it out.

CHAIM WEIZMANN

History is always best written generations after the event, when clouded fact and memory have all fused into what can be accepted as truth, whether it be so or not.

THEODORE H. WHITE

A Jew is someone who ties, who links his or her destiny to the Jewish people. Period. This is a Jew. I do not enter religious affairs.

ELIE WIESEL

A certain columnist has been barred from all Shubert openings. Now he can wait three days and go to their closings.

Optimist—A man who gets treed by a lion but enjoys the scenery.

WALTER WINCHELL

I would rather think of my religion as a gamble than to think of it as an insurance policy.

STEPHEN S. WISE

When a poor man eats a chicken, one or the other is sick.

Approach a goat from the back, a horse from the front, and a stupid man from no direction whatsoever.

"For example" is not proof.

When a father gives to his son, both laugh. When a son gives to his father, both cry.

The girl who can't dance says the band can't play.

If a dealt in candles, the sun would never set.

Don't ask the doctor, ask the patient.

If the rich could hire other people to die for them, the poor could make a wonderful living.

Come for your inheritance and you may have to pay for the funeral.

YIDDISH PROVERBS

My grandmother is over eighty and still doesn't need glasses. Drinks right out of the bottle.

Bore—a guy with a cocktail glass in one hand and your lapel in the other.

My wife has a slight impediment in her speech. Every once in a while she stops to breathe.

HENNY YOUNGMAN

The average taxpayer is no more capable of a "grand passion" than of grand opera.

The Jews are a frightened people. Nineteen centuries of Christian love have broken down their nerves.

Indifference and hypocrisy between them keep orthodoxy alive.

Selfishness is the only real atheism; aspiration, unselfishness, the only real religion.

Let us start a new religion with one commandment, "Enjoy thyself."

Every dogma has its day, but ideals are eternal.

America is God's Crucible, the great Melting-Pot where all the races of Europe are melting and reforming! . . . God is making the American.

The only true love is love at first sight; second sight dispels it.

The way [George Bernard] Shaw believes in himself is very refreshing in these atheistic times when so many believe in no God at all.

The Jews remained a chosen race, a peculiar people, faulty enough, but redeemed at least from the grosser vices—a little human islet won from the waters of animalism by the genius of ancient engineers.

ISRAEL ZANGWILL

DOVER · THRIFT · EDITIONS

POETRY

A SHROPSHIRE LAD, A. E. Housman. 64pp. 26468-8 $1.00

LYRIC POEMS, John Keats. 80pp. 26871-3 $1.00

GUNGA DIN AND OTHER FAVORITE POEMS, Rudyard Kipling. 80pp. 26471-8 $1.00

THE CONGO AND OTHER POEMS, Vachel Lindsay. 96pp. 27272-9 $1.50

EVANGELINE AND OTHER POEMS, Henry Wadsworth Longfellow. 64pp. 28255-4 $1.00

FAVORITE POEMS, Henry Wadsworth Longfellow. 96pp. 27273-7 $1.00

"TO HIS COY MISTRESS" AND OTHER POEMS, Andrew Marvell. 64pp. 29544-3 $1.00

SPOON RIVER ANTHOLOGY, Edgar Lee Masters. 144pp. 27275-3 $1.50

RENASCENCE AND OTHER POEMS, Edna St. Vincent Millay. 64pp. (Available in U.S. only.) 26873-X $1.00

SELECTED POEMS, John Milton. 128pp. 27554-X $1.50

CIVIL WAR POETRY: An Anthology, Paul Negri (ed.). 128pp. 29883-3 $1.50

ENGLISH VICTORIAN POETRY: AN ANTHOLOGY, Paul Negri (ed.). 256pp. 40425-0 $2.00

GREAT SONNETS, Paul Negri (ed.). 96pp. 28052-7 $1.00

THE RAVEN AND OTHER FAVORITE POEMS, Edgar Allan Poe. 64pp. 26685-0 $1.00

ESSAY ON MAN AND OTHER POEMS, Alexander Pope. 128pp. 28053-5 $1.50

EARLY POEMS, Ezra Pound. 80pp. (Available in U.S. only.) 28745-9 $1.00

GREAT POEMS BY AMERICAN WOMEN: An Anthology, Susan L. Rattiner (ed.). 224pp. (Available in U.S. only.) 40164-2 $2.00

LITTLE ORPHANT ANNIE AND OTHER POEMS, James Whitcomb Riley. 80pp. 28260-0 $1.00

"MINIVER CHEEVY" AND OTHER POEMS, Edwin Arlington Robinson. 64pp. 28756-4 $1.00

GOBLIN MARKET AND OTHER POEMS, Christina Rossetti. 64pp. 28055-1 $1.00

CHICAGO POEMS, Carl Sandburg. 80pp. 28057-8 $1.00

THE SHOOTING OF DAN MCGREW AND OTHER POEMS, Robert Service. 96pp. (Available in U.S. only.) 27556-6 $1.50

COMPLETE SONNETS, William Shakespeare. 80pp. 26686-9 $1.00

SELECTED POEMS, Percy Bysshe Shelley. 128pp. 27558-2 $1.50

AFRICAN-AMERICAN POETRY: An Anthology, 1773–1930, Joan R. Sherman (ed.). 96pp. 29604-0 $1.00

100 BEST-LOVED POEMS, Philip Smith (ed.). 96pp. 28553-7 $1.00

NATIVE AMERICAN SONGS AND POEMS: An Anthology, Brian Swann (ed.). 64pp. 29450-1 $1.00

SELECTED POEMS, Alfred Lord Tennyson. 112pp. 27282-6 $1.50

AENEID, Vergil (Publius Vergilius Maro). 256pp. 28749-1 $2.00

CHRISTMAS CAROLS: COMPLETE VERSES, Shane Weller (ed.). 64pp. 27397-0 $1.00

GREAT LOVE POEMS, Shane Weller (ed.). 128pp. 27284-2 $1.00

CIVIL WAR POETRY AND PROSE, Walt Whitman. 96pp. 28507-3 $1.00

SELECTED POEMS, Walt Whitman. 128pp. 26878-0 $1.00

THE BALLAD OF READING GAOL AND OTHER POEMS, Oscar Wilde. 64pp. 27072-6 $1.00

EARLY POEMS, William Carlos Williams. 64pp. (Available in U.S. only.) 29294-0 $1.00

FAVORITE POEMS, William Wordsworth. 80pp. 27073-4 $1.00

WORLD WAR ONE BRITISH POETS: Brooke, Owen, Sassoon, Rosenberg, and Others, Candace Ward (ed.). (Available in U.S. only.) 29568-0 $1.00

EARLY POEMS, William Butler Yeats. 128pp. 27808-5 $1.50

"EASTER, 1916" AND OTHER POEMS, William Butler Yeats. 80pp. (Available in U.S. only.) 29771-3 $1.00

DOVER·THRIFT·EDITIONS

FICTION

FLATLAND: A ROMANCE OF MANY DIMENSIONS, Edwin A. Abbott. 96pp. 27263-X $1.00

SHORT STORIES, Louisa May Alcott. 64pp. 29063-8 $1.00

WINESBURG, OHIO, Sherwood Anderson. 160pp. 28269-4 $2.00

PERSUASION, Jane Austen. 224pp. 29555-9 $2.00

PRIDE AND PREJUDICE, Jane Austen. 272pp. 28473-5 $2.00

SENSE AND SENSIBILITY, Jane Austen. 272pp. 29049-2 $2.00

LOOKING BACKWARD, Edward Bellamy. 160pp. 29038-7 $2.00

BEOWULF, Beowulf (trans. by R. K. Gordon). 64pp. 27264-8 $1.00

CIVIL WAR STORIES, Ambrose Bierce. 128pp. 28038-1 $1.00

"THE MOONLIT ROAD" AND OTHER GHOST AND HORROR STORIES, Ambrose Bierce (John Grafton, ed.) 96pp. 40056-5 $1.00

WUTHERING HEIGHTS, Emily Brontë. 256pp. 29256-8 $2.00

THE THIRTY-NINE STEPS, John Buchan. 96pp. 28201-5 $1.50

TARZAN OF THE APES, Edgar Rice Burroughs. 224pp. (Available in U.S. only.) 29570-2 $2.00

ALICE'S ADVENTURES IN WONDERLAND, Lewis Carroll. 96pp. 27543-4 $1.00

THROUGH THE LOOKING-GLASS, Lewis Carroll. 128pp. 40878-7 $1.50

MY ÁNTONIA, Willa Cather. 176pp. 28240-6 $2.00

O PIONEERS!, Willa Cather. 128pp. 27785-2 $1.00

PAUL'S CASE AND OTHER STORIES, Willa Cather. 64pp. 29057-3 $1.00

FIVE GREAT SHORT STORIES, Anton Chekhov. 96pp. 26463-7 $1.00

TALES OF CONJURE AND THE COLOR LINE, Charles Waddell Chesnutt. 128pp. 40426-9 $1.50

FAVORITE FATHER BROWN STORIES, G. K. Chesterton. 96pp. 27545-0 $1.00

THE AWAKENING, Kate Chopin. 128pp. 27786-0 $1.00

A PAIR OF SILK STOCKINGS AND OTHER STORIES, Kate Chopin. 64pp. 29264-9 $1.00

HEART OF DARKNESS, Joseph Conrad. 80pp. 26464-5 $1.00

LORD JIM, Joseph Conrad. 256pp. 40650-4 $2.00

THE SECRET SHARER AND OTHER STORIES, Joseph Conrad. 128pp. 27546-9 $1.00

THE "LITTLE REGIMENT" AND OTHER CIVIL WAR STORIES, Stephen Crane. 80pp. 29557-5 $1.00

THE OPEN BOAT AND OTHER STORIES, Stephen Crane. 128pp. 27547-7 $1.50

THE RED BADGE OF COURAGE, Stephen Crane. 112pp. 26465-3 $1.00

MOLL FLANDERS, Daniel Defoe. 256pp. 29093-X $2.00

ROBINSON CRUSOE, Daniel Defoe. 288pp. 40427-7 $2.00

A CHRISTMAS CAROL, Charles Dickens. 80pp. 26865-9 $1.00

THE CRICKET ON THE HEARTH AND OTHER CHRISTMAS STORIES, Charles Dickens. 128pp. 28039-X $1.00

A TALE OF TWO CITIES, Charles Dickens. 304pp. 40651-2 $2.00

THE DOUBLE, Fyodor Dostoyevsky. 128pp. 29572-9 $1.50

THE GAMBLER, Fyodor Dostoyevsky. 112pp. 29081-6 $1.50

NOTES FROM THE UNDERGROUND, Fyodor Dostoyevsky. 96pp. 27053-X $1.00

THE ADVENTURE OF THE DANCING MEN AND OTHER STORIES, Sir Arthur Conan Doyle. 80pp. 29558-3 $1.00

THE HOUND OF THE BASKERVILLES, Arthur Conan Doyle. 128pp. 28214-7 $1.50

THE LOST WORLD, Arthur Conan Doyle. 176pp. 40060-3 $1.50

DOVER · THRIFT · EDITIONS

FICTION

SIX GREAT SHERLOCK HOLMES STORIES, Sir Arthur Conan Doyle. 112pp. 27055-6 $1.00

SILAS MARNER, George Eliot. 160pp. 29246-0 $1.50

THIS SIDE OF PARADISE, F. Scott Fitzgerald. 208pp. 28999-0 $2.00

"THE DIAMOND AS BIG AS THE RITZ" AND OTHER STORIES, F. Scott Fitzgerald. 29991-0 $2.00

THE REVOLT OF "MOTHER" AND OTHER STORIES, Mary E. Wilkins Freeman. 128pp. 40428-5 $1.50

MADAME BOVARY, Gustave Flaubert. 256pp. 29257-6 $2.00

WHERE ANGELS FEAR TO TREAD, E. M. Forster. 128pp. (Available in U.S. only.) 27791-7 $1.50

A ROOM WITH A VIEW, E. M. Forster. 176pp. (Available in U.S. only.) 28467-0 $2.00

THE IMMORALIST, André Gide. 112pp. (Available in U.S. only.) 29237-1 $1.50

"THE YELLOW WALLPAPER" AND OTHER STORIES, Charlotte Perkins Gilman. 80pp. 29857-4 $1.00

HERLAND, Charlotte Perkins Gilman. 128pp. 40429-3 $1.50

THE OVERCOAT AND OTHER STORIES, Nikolai Gogol. 112pp. 27057-2 $1.50

GREAT GHOST STORIES, John Grafton (ed.). 112pp. 27270-2 $1.00

DETECTION BY GASLIGHT, Douglas G. Greene (ed.). 272pp. 29928-7 $2.00

THE MABINOGION, Lady Charlotte E. Guest. 192pp. 29541-9 $2.00

"THE FIDDLER OF THE REELS" AND OTHER SHORT STORIES, Thomas Hardy. 80pp. 29960-0 $1.50

THE LUCK OF ROARING CAMP AND OTHER STORIES, Bret Harte. 96pp. 27271-0 $1.00

THE SCARLET LETTER, Nathaniel Hawthorne. 192pp. 28048-9 $2.00

YOUNG GOODMAN BROWN AND OTHER STORIES, Nathaniel Hawthorne. 128pp. 27060-2 $1.00

THE GIFT OF THE MAGI AND OTHER SHORT STORIES, O. Henry. 96pp. 27061-0 $1.00

THE NUTCRACKER AND THE GOLDEN POT, E. T. A. Hoffmann. 128pp. 27806-9 $1.00

THE BEAST IN THE JUNGLE AND OTHER STORIES, Henry James. 128pp. 27552-3 $1.50

DAISY MILLER, Henry James. 64pp. 28773-4 $1.00

THE TURN OF THE SCREW, Henry James. 96pp. 26684-2 $1.00

WASHINGTON SQUARE, Henry James. 176pp. 40431-5 $2.00

THE COUNTRY OF THE POINTED FIRS, Sarah Orne Jewett. 96pp. 28196-5 $1.00

THE AUTOBIOGRAPHY OF AN EX-COLORED MAN, James Weldon Johnson. 112pp. 28512-X $1.00

DUBLINERS, James Joyce. 160pp. 26870-5 $1.00

A PORTRAIT OF THE ARTIST AS A YOUNG MAN, James Joyce. 192pp. 28050-0 $2.00

THE METAMORPHOSIS AND OTHER STORIES, Franz Kafka. 96pp. 29030-1 $1.50

THE MAN WHO WOULD BE KING AND OTHER STORIES, Rudyard Kipling. 128pp. 28051-9 $1.50

YOU KNOW ME AL, Ring Lardner. 128pp. 28513-8 $1.50

SELECTED SHORT STORIES, D. H. Lawrence. 128pp. 27794-1 $1.50

GREEN TEA AND OTHER GHOST STORIES, J. Sheridan LeFanu. 96pp. 27795-X $1.50

SHORT STORIES, Theodore Dreiser. 112pp. 28215-5 $1.50

THE CALL OF THE WILD, Jack London. 64pp. 26472-6 $1.00

FIVE GREAT SHORT STORIES, Jack London. 96pp. 27063-7 $1.00

WHITE FANG, Jack London. 160pp. 26968-X $1.00

DEATH IN VENICE, Thomas Mann. 96pp. (Available in U.S. only.) 28714-9 $1.00

IN A GERMAN PENSION: 13 Stories, Katherine Mansfield. 112pp. 28719-X $1.50

THE MOON AND SIXPENCE, W. Somerset Maugham. 176pp. (Available in U.S. only.) 28731-9 $2.00

DOVER · THRIFT · EDITIONS

FICTION

THE NECKLACE AND OTHER SHORT STORIES, Guy de Maupassant. 128pp. 27064-5 $1.00
BARTLEBY AND BENITO CERENO, Herman Melville. 112pp. 26473-4 $1.00
THE OIL JAR AND OTHER STORIES, Luigi Pirandello. 96pp. 28459-X $1.00
THE GOLD-BUG AND OTHER TALES, Edgar Allan Poe. 128pp. 26875-6 $1.00
TALES OF TERROR AND DETECTION, Edgar Allan Poe. 96pp. 28744-0 $1.00
THE QUEEN OF SPADES AND OTHER STORIES, Alexander Pushkin. 128pp. 28054-3 $1.50
SREDNI VASHTAR AND OTHER STORIES, Saki (H. H. Munro). 96pp. 28521-9 $1.00
THE STORY OF AN AFRICAN FARM, Olive Schreiner. 256pp. 40165-0 $2.00
FRANKENSTEIN, Mary Shelley. 176pp. 28211-2 $1.00
THREE LIVES, Gertrude Stein. 176pp. (Available in U.S. only.) 28059-4 $2.00
THE STRANGE CASE OF DR. JEKYLL AND MR. HYDE, Robert Louis Stevenson. 64pp. 26688-5 $1.00
TREASURE ISLAND, Robert Louis Stevenson. 160pp. 27559-0 $1.50
GULLIVER'S TRAVELS, Jonathan Swift. 240pp. 29273-8 $2.00
THE KREUTZER SONATA AND OTHER SHORT STORIES, Leo Tolstoy. 144pp. 27805-0 $1.50
THE WARDEN, Anthony Trollope. 176pp. 40076-X $2.00
FIRST LOVE AND DIARY OF A SUPERFLUOUS MAN, Ivan Turgenev. 96pp. 28775-0 $1.50
FATHERS AND SONS, Ivan Turgenev. 176pp. 40073-5 $2.00
ADVENTURES OF HUCKLEBERRY FINN, Mark Twain. 224pp. 28061-6 $2.00
THE ADVENTURES OF TOM SAWYER, Mark Twain. 192pp. 40077-8 $2.00
THE MYSTERIOUS STRANGER AND OTHER STORIES, Mark Twain. 128pp. 27069-6 $1.00
HUMOROUS STORIES AND SKETCHES, Mark Twain. 80pp. 29279-7 $1.00
CANDIDE, Voltaire (François-Marie Arouet). 112pp. 26689-3 $1.00
GREAT SHORT STORIES BY AMERICAN WOMEN, Candace Ward (ed.). 192pp. 28776-9 $2.00
"THE COUNTRY OF THE BLIND" AND OTHER SCIENCE-FICTION STORIES, H. G. Wells. 160pp. (Available in U.S. only.) 29569-9 $1.00
THE ISLAND OF DR. MOREAU, H. G. Wells. 112pp. (Available in U.S. only.) 29027-1 $1.50
THE INVISIBLE MAN, H. G. Wells. 112pp. (Available in U.S. only.) 27071-8 $1.00
THE TIME MACHINE, H. G. Wells. 80pp. (Available in U.S. only.) 28472-7 $1.00
THE WAR OF THE WORLDS, H. G. Wells. 160pp. (Available in U.S. only.) 29506-0 $1.00
ETHAN FROME, Edith Wharton. 96pp. 26690-7 $1.00
SHORT STORIES, Edith Wharton. 128pp. 28235-X $1.50
THE AGE OF INNOCENCE, Edith Wharton. 288pp. 29803-5 $2.00
THE PICTURE OF DORIAN GRAY, Oscar Wilde. 192pp. 27807-7 $1.50
JACOB'S ROOM, Virginia Woolf. 144pp. (Available in U.S. only.) 40109-X $1.50
MONDAY OR TUESDAY: Eight Stories, Virginia Woolf. 64pp. (Available in U.S. only.) 29453-6 $1.00

NONFICTION

POETICS, Aristotle. 64pp. 29577-X $1.00
NICOMACHEAN ETHICS, Aristotle. 256pp. 40096-4 $2.00
MEDITATIONS, Marcus Aurelius. 128pp. 29823-X $1.50
THE LAND OF LITTLE RAIN, Mary Austin. 96pp. 29037-9 $1.50
THE DEVIL'S DICTIONARY, Ambrose Bierce. 144pp. 27542-6 $1.00
THE ANALECTS, Confucius. 128pp. 28484-0 $2.00
CONFESSIONS OF AN ENGLISH OPIUM EATER, Thomas De Quincey. 80pp. 28742-4 $1.00
NARRATIVE OF THE LIFE OF FREDERICK DOUGLASS, Frederick Douglass. 96pp. 28499-9 $1.00